Nothing True Has a Name

Critical Praise for the books of Djelloul Marbrook

Artemisia's Wolf (title story in *A Warding Circle*)

... successfully blends humor and satire (and perhaps even a touch of magic realism) into its short length ... an engrossing story, but what might strike the reader most throughout the book is its infusion of breathtaking poetry... a stunning rebuke to notoriously misogynist subcultures like the New York art scene, showing us just how hard it is for a young woman to be judged on her creative talent alone.

—Tommy Zurhellen, *Hudson River Valley Review*

Saraceno

... Djelloul Marbrook writes dialogue that not only entertains with an intoxicating clickety-clack, but also packs a truth about low-life mob culture *The Sopranos* only hints at. You can practically smell the anisette and filling-station coffee.

—Dan Baum, author of *Gun Guys* (2013), *Nine Lives: Mystery, Magic, Death and Life in New Orleans* (2009) and others

... a good ear for crackling dialogue ... I love Marbrook's crude, raw music of the streets. The notes are authentic and on target ...

—Sam Coale, *The Providence (RI) Journal*

... an entirely new variety of gangster tale ... a Mafia story sculpted with the most refined of sensibilities from the clay of high art and philosophy ... the kind of writer I take real pleasure in discovering ... a mature artist whose rich body of work is finally coming to light.

—Brent Robison, editor, *Prima Materia*

Far from Algiers

... as succinct as most stanzas by Dickinson... an unusually mature, confidently composed first poetry collection.

—Susanna Roxman, *Prairie Schooner*

... brings together the energy of a young poet with the wisdom of long experience.

—Edward Hirsch, Guggenheim Foundation

Brushstrokes and Glances

Whether it is commentary on state power, corporate greed, or the intensely personal death of a loved one, Djelloul Marbrook is clear-sighted, eloquent, and precise. As the title of the collection suggests, he uses the lightest touch, a collection of fragments, brushstrokes and glances, to fashion poems that resonate with truth and honesty.

—Phil Constable, *New York Journal of Books*

Nothing True Has a Name

poems by

Djelloul Marbrook

LEAKY BOOT PRESS

Nothing True Has a Name
by Djelloul Marbrook

Acknowledgments

"Dye run" was published by
Deep Water Literary Journal, No. 2, 2014

First published in 2017 by
Leaky Boot Press
http://www.leakyboot.com

ISBN: 978-1-909849-22-8

All goodnesses should be nameless.

—Mehmet Murat Ilda

To all I read in strangers' eyes.

Contents

Proem

Sailing in dry river beds

Now to write with what was burned

Ambitions larger than Alexander's

Silver halide

What is more

Too big, too loud, too bright

Proem

A time of desperate purity

I

The wrong word can save your life,
abort a hundred complications,
and in a time of desperate purity
ward off the daemon bearing
your death in her scented bosom.

You scare me, he said, and she left
because he was supposed to say
words of such inconsequence
that would make him easy prey.
She could not rise to the challenge

And so he was free to walk away.
Simple truth is hard to come by,
life sets in while you suck your thumbs,
but once in a while the word comes out
and nothing is ever familiar again.

II

To know something about astrophysics is to know
from no distance is it safe to love you. I and they
can never go that distance, club-footed as they are,
only the second person, eternal addressee, can use
worlds as stepping stones and not look back because
you're always getting to where you've always been
and all the forests of I and dens of they are no-see-ums
to the flashing ankles of the sprite who explores
undiscovered planets while making love to you.

Sailing in
dry river beds

Nothing true

Take my fantasies to Cockaigne
in amphorae lashed by the neck
to the hold of a sewn ship
& then, captain, set your sails

for where there be dragons,
rocs & the perils of desire;
I want no profit from it.
I've become black wind itself

stirring pretense of home.
I huff my fantasies out to sea
to see what is left of me;
that's all that's left to do

but turn my back on everyone
to greet the dread companion
whose whisperings have finally
come within my decibel range:

Ahoy, Beloved, I'm here & now
& know nothing true has a name.

Sailing in dry river beds

is treason against the waking state—
short-haul in navels of goddesses,
set spinnakers in dry stream beds,
round star-buoys in the Milky Way,
criminal in an inner circle
of family and friends,
assassin whose life now depends
on paranoia that picks the faces off
people who smile at you
wondering what it will take
to founder you tonight,
waving their wreckers' lanterns
until you break up on their knees
and they loot the laboratory
of your dreams
swilling from this and that,
drunk on you, not noticing
you walking towards the dunes.

Ocracoke

Red-light the compass, red-light the charts,
I can't lose my night vision navigating you,
your shoals, shifting wrecks, sand bars.

All that's not me is you; third person
is a pigeonhole and a putting off
to save us from grappling with one another.

Every one of us hides in Ocracoke and flies
another country's colors, but what
is in your hold is always what I'm after.

Mad anchoring

One green week in May the lighthouse drifted closer,
Mutual Fun and For Play left such a bloody wake
the dockmaster called me to investigate and I concluded
leviathan had been caught in the props
and there was nothing to worry about a little tinkering
of the amplitudhedron wouldn't fix
and I would get on it right away.

I say right away when I mean tomorrow
because an idea is a stopcock from which energy escapes
if you talk about it. That's all exhibitionism is,
mad anchoring so as not to flow back and forth between
this and the other lives we're still living. Tomorrow
I'll polish this particular facet of the jewel.

This first person about whom I speak, you might think him God
or me delusional, but I mean we're all collaborators
doing and undoing, making and unmaking the world.
Nothing is left behind, no one is left behind, & if I say
the lighthouse will wash up here it will in my universe
if not yours. Best we grasp this before becoming androgynes.

You who were not let in are chosen

to sail in paper ships, board derelicts,
fit them out again, eat bugs, kill inspectors.

Without local knowledge you sound your way
through shallows, consort with dragons,
arrive at the ultimate horror: nothing is ever over.

Dream in thunder

Leave the sirens to creaking moor lines,
torches and rutters written in blood. Leave
purposes, sundries and flagging hope
and step ashore to walk with me.

At dawn I will let you go,
but I want to talk to you
about friends who do not wish you well.
You've stayed too long, they think,

disappointed them with your successes,
not that you were meant to go to hell
but simply not succeed. Instead,
you've written poems, kept promises

and made a nuisance of yourself.
I want you to go back and kill them
with whetted scythe, despair,
and when you come to me again

signal from the yardarm that for once
your face is tired of your smile.

Betrayal

Death is betrayal
not of the dead but of the living
who cannot grip the vacuum
left in odium and/or love
betrayal
worst than jerking into life
a kind of waking
from wherewithal understood
a burning until unknowing
like a Viking longboat bearing
the corpse we're born to be
down to the sea of phantom pilings
to which we hitch our guises
goodbye you me and our supposed inferences
up in flames at the mouth of the fjord
goodbye to our pretenses
that we found handholds in the vacuum
goodbye to this hollow hello
we could not hallow
and any assurance we had
that even hatred would last
long enough to cook a meal
or sing a broken song
betrayal
birth is betrayal too

Like a ship's prow

That is perhaps why you are smiling

because you cut like a ship's prow
let me guess this about you

nothing sticks to you and you are naked
on the dressiest of occasions

because you find us itchy
& would rather fuck icicles

than endure our whining
but I could be wrong and if I am

that is perhaps why you are smiling

One immune to Helen's face

I saw Helen's face
turn the ships back

it was an awful mistake
that gods made such a smile
men could no longer trust them

Turned ideologies to piss
made sailors laugh so hard
they farted triremes home

The Greeks made up stories
about what happened
that shaped civilizations

I like the Brothers Grimm better
to be scared than full of shit

You think the Greeks were any more honest
about their reasons for going to war
than the Americans in Iraq?

I saw Helen's face
and I wanted to say
it should have been unlawful

Woulda shoulda coulda
has it ever occurred to you
that nothing you have to say
is half as important as
the space you take to say it in?

Say it on?

In the bone in the marrow
you have always wanted to get in

      I'm a sorry lockpick
      I'll give you that
      I know very little else I know
      & I'm only doing this
      saying this in hope...

    someone will intervene
   one on whom names fail to stick,
  a third rail without which the other two
   are fingers pointing to where...

to where no one wants to go.
Sorry. Sorry, will I do?

      No, you and I are locked
      in a duet in which the dots
      do anything to be connected
      except the one thing
      poems and sweat endeavors
      are about

      You will not do

And neither will you
& there we are
needing one on whom names fail to stick...

    one immune to Helen's face

Limn a line from a sporran of moss

to the patinaed handle of your mind
dispatch a cutter close-hauled & fuming
down this fjord to Atlantis
where the daemons you have met
wait to frisk her hold for emeralds
& all the rare-earth minerals
you create by this simple act

This is what prayer is like
                          not witness
but close observation of a kind
that inflames each thought
with a divine disease that burns
the red wounds of memories off
& leaves the creature you have made
to mislead your trackers in the woods

Before it was stolen away

Authority is anything remotely resembling sea swell,
all else is commotion in a bottle, not
to be trusted, and a life lived as a whale,
whatever deceptive form it takes, is better
than bearing things from one place to another
and yammering about its importance.

I only pretend to know this or else remember
a time when I did—hiraeth
where I was behemoth and played
with the ancient light of stars as it illumined
memories swimming by, played like a child
before paradise was stolen away.

By the time the Navy gave me glasses

I don't belong here as much as you do
or you or you or you
I testify I do
it's fortunate I couldn't see too much
but I remember her smell
and by the time the Navy gave me glasses
it was much too late
for anything
anything like belonging
trusting or setting foot
on terra firma
home ground
a place by the hearth
anything like that
which might have implied belonging
or having belongings
to satisfy longings to which I had no right

Navel of Marmara

My cataracts do not veil
your estuarine scent,
my nose undresses you
and in the navel of Marmara
vessels wheel that bear
ideas to Greek Islands,
amphorae of hope, kraters
brimming headiness, hubris
sewn in stacks. They twirl
counterclockwise stirred
by idle goddesses' tits,
and I pretend to sleep
so as not to be suspected
of containing this,
of being that one vial
demons left someone to open
and you to wonder if
you are that one.

Dragging anchor

If life is a near-death experiment
is death dread of living again,
are words adequate instruments
to cut the fierce cyst of delusion
from our bodies allowing us
calm in which to calculate
the consequence of trampling
wet petals never seen before?

No time to meet someone to trust,
yet we must take it dead or alive
so that in some better state
we'll need no words to paint
thoughts across our mirrored faces.

What do I know but that talking
keeps me from going mad,
what do I know but being mad
is what keeps me talking?
I know what pirates know,
I know that having a name
is to drag an anchor across the sea
of malevolence under false colors.

Now to write with what has burned

Now to write with what has burned

I

I am a genderless noun
adoring extremely you
contemptuous of I girders
the et cetera of they

In the tsunami of you
I sort pronounal debris
& you are the only one
I do not give back to the sea

You are natural geometry
always deciding what to be
not right angles breaking off
& corners collecting dust

I am through collecting dusk
with impenetrable personae
I have run clean out of me
kindling the kiln of you

II

The thingness of a thing
is the fall of its cloak
the distance of the fall
the number of its lumens
and its penetrability

The I in I am is a scalpel
its passage an offense
against the settled idea
the thingness of a thing
abandoning its attachments—

death belying everything
we have said about it

The word disappears

The stress in the word disappears
conceals from us the fact
nothing does.

We can't stress appears,
so we say a person's gone
because for wishing someone dead

we're not prepared to pay
but we do pay with our fear
that we've wished someone away.

I know who you are, you know I know
and that I will go on knowing
when you say I disappeared

Wouldn't it be better to admit we're made
of everyone else who ever lived
on earths we've yet to find

and that they've found us
and shower us with the light
to help us find our way?

Not whom I liked

If visual logic could be trusted,
if decisions were right-angled,
if my mind sounded like Bach,
Mozart subversive, Stravinsky nihilistic,
if I trusted my antennae
and not whom I liked
I'd be the person I came to be
in spite of my best efforts
to be someone else, someone
who smiled more and called up friends,
someone you trusted against
all the evidence of your senses,
someone like you perhaps.
If you asked me more I'd say
my poems best not go on.

Number 20

My facial recognition software
says you're number 20 on a list
of suspects in the bombing
of my memory palace, so
I don't know whether to co-operate
with the authorities because
I can't remember your significance.
Usually I can't remember a name,
but I remember trouble or love,
foreboding, longing, scent,
flight or the instant I should have fled
and sometimes I don't want to say
who I've recognized for fear
of having to live over again
the reasons I'm misshapen,
but once in a while they fall across my face,
ones who drew my breath, and I
am noctilucent in the heat
of summer's remembering.

I see what thoughts become

wrapping their tails around words,
pawing them on the carpet
between us. Who is the creature,
the thinker or the thought?
I see what thoughts become:
enigma, weather, disease,
golem made of history's parts,
Maimonides, calculus, condiment,
caliph, vizier, god & trees.

Convicted of a treasonable stare,
I am flayed & hung on hooks.
They see me coming & tell you
whether to speak or shelter them
from my omnivorous eye.

You rarely take their advice,
being second person to their first,
and I watch them scurry,
tails disappearing under beds,
tracking blood on ceilings,
passages of light in cracks,
dampnesses that do not dry.

I see their unearthliness,
evil, grandeur & fear
of being discovered by beasts
who take them for you & me.

I see them steal my words from you
to make better use of them
& as I die I finally confess
they're the ones I care about,
my countrymen & conspirators.

I hold them sacred because they know
all gifts are curses in disguise.
There is no hell but this & heaven
is that one thing they have not become.

The quarry

You words are on your own
not that I have set you free
but that in your avoidance of me
you have wandered from the maze
where I was peeing on the roses
and now have galactic garbage dumps
and needy civilizations to explore.

Here is your opportunity to mean
idiots-know-what and get away
with uninvented crimes
that haven't even been given names
and all because you rightly saw
I meant to push you into the quarry,
but you smiled and sang a hymn of no.

A man who sets his words free
takes his chances with chaos
or simply recognizes he never owned them,
but as his glances changed their objects
words worked with him a little while,
worked him and made him malleable
to algorithms light-years getting here.

I don't know what to say now that I go
to live a life that testifies to that.

Dervish

My business is being gone
not in embossed letters
or anything like that, gone
beyond thought of home
or anyone's imagining,
gone beyond former self
and the trouble of it, gone
to where there be dragons,
roses enclosing galaxies,
ecstatic loneliness.

My business is being gone
not gone to you or lost
or absent or due back
but in the intimate moment
gone to history, gone to self,
as impossible a task
as a da Vinci or Raphael.

It's a shame to talk about it,
a hesitancy, but some of us
are cursed to recollect
in order to go on,
go on to being gone.

Dervish prayer

You don't know how you're going to feel,
there's no immunity from the elixirs of the place,
and the moment is so whimsical only fools
trust it not to turn them inside out.
If you risk genuine response
nobody will know you in the morning
and, better yet, they'll all be strangers.
Let's not spend our lives pretending
we don't have each other's number.

From the fury of those who do the math,
good Lord, deliver us, and in the glory of doing it
may we burn up and disappear.

That day

This world is my word's shadow.
I stepped out from it once
and in the white madness spoke
a language I'm trying to remember
so that I may speak to you again,
you nobles who didn't choose to look like us,
whose names remain out of decibel range,
outside the door of my machinery,
you gods who comforted me
that day I bled and cast no shadow.

Ambitions larger than Alexander's

Ambitions larger than Alexander's

I have ambitions larger than Alexander's.
I want mirrors to give up their secrets
because they trust me, I want
to wipe away the matter that causes
you to twinkle instead of emitting
steady light. I want to see
all the facets of the jewel at once,
I want to enclose as much as I am enclosed,
I want to know how each elixir tastes
before it ennobles elements, I want
to sin in this preposterous way
and be forgiven for making alien creatures
laugh so hard their stealth material
falls off and we see horrors too glorious
to deny, I want to explain this to Alexander
in a way that inspires him to forgo
his regrets about burning Persepolis down.

You

Exude, dehisce, encapsulate,
I savor it all,
sometimes overcome in my laboratory
by discoveries I can't repeat.

I hear the cries of plants, the independent
pleas of drops of sweat & blood,
I'm drunk on the tears of trees.

Exude, dehisce, encapsulate
the whirling dervishes of our senses
riveting the audience of the mind.

I knew I'd have to make up stories,
I'd have to pretend I could filter
their excrescences, and if they made me sick
I'd have to pretend I was grateful
for their half-ass cures & vaccines,
but all I'm really grateful for
is being such a stubborn savoror.

I exude, you dehisce,
between us we encapsulate
deals that rig currencies
of a pastime world that passes
for reality, while drunk we drive
ourselves to distraction wondering

what's really going on and dreading
the answer might be within ourselves
ready to explode all over the second person
society exists to hold at bay.

Losing it

With which dimension are you fragrant today,
have you shed it enough to operate here,
and where is here, or there, and who
am I or you? I think a good start might be
to stop pretending that we know, to sound
the depths of our ignorance and take comfort
in all there is to learn even if it means
getting lost on the way to our pretended home.

If art is about reach beyond the pale,
any pale, how in good conscience, how
in decency can we speak learnedly about it?

Credentials should attest what we don't know
and if they did our humility would prize
the dimensions open and our kinds
would be jubilant and constellate.

Buzzards circling

Oh and then because
of the whatnot of it all
I saw buzzards circling
the hunter and he looked
at me as if I could
do something about it
but the sun was setting
and I said perhaps
if you were to put your shotgun down
you would look less
like roadkill and more
like something living once
and they would go away
or you could take another swig
and try to get a signal
from your cheating wife
and I could write this down
for will-o'-the-wisp and marsh hens

The antidote

I have drawn the harm from you
to look without flinching
even when you purported to be dead
but you are not in my debt
because I didn't drink for you
the arsenic of your compulsion
to be offended   I drank
in the sure conviction one of us
would survive the antidote
of the other and be reborn
imbued with a still memory
of our celebrated folly

300-dpi embodiment

Headlong in a frame of your screen
crucified by your crosshairs
I am the 300-dpi embodiment
of the figments that elude you
and it is no comfort to me
I come over you like malaria
reminding you of some tropic din
red and insectful of where you've been
no comfort to you I am sure that this time
something good will come of our chagrin

You, this instant

You are the untold climax arriving
after millennia of travel, and I
am the gauge of my knowledge of it.
I stalk your scent in the night heavens,
follow your footprints in the seas—
you, untold blasts inviting me
to be your gardener, to mind
your arabesques of raptures
as if they were mine, and in return
you are my lightning illuminating
futures before they turn creaturely,
before my gaze carves them,
and in your instant I live and die.

Some corners

Did I choose you to befall me,
wrap you in a lie of complaint,
or did you trip me as I turned a corner
and then come to my assistance
as if you just happened to be standing there?

Some corners are better left unturned.

Gas giants gather in this room

My meridians and parallels are not settled matters.
Like history, your cartography lies
for the convenience of commerce, leaving me
to shake off your profitable illnesses,
reaffirm my incorporeality and count
my moons while you insist I'm as solid
& fixed as you are in your ignorance.

Gas giants, ice giants, gather in this room
to be misunderstood by experts and work
the cryptography of the stars. You must get by me
to understand your lives as mites.
I am your political entertainment,
I distract you from your tragedy,
I deter you on your way to glory.

Jupiter, your sixty-seven moons are dandruff
on the shoulders of the galaxy. Uranus,
wear your rings and shifty robes as indifferent
to the messages of the stars as you have been,
as I have been. Too content with our galaxies,
our thick skins brush off the arias
of light-years exhorting us to expand.

Savoring your prickliness

Between my Neanderthal genes
and face-blind dreams
a world emerges

What am I doing here
in dreams between the cracks
of something unfolding on Sirius?

Good thing I can smell you
and savor your prickliness,
but your fragrances repel me

Continents are eliding,
pushing up strange flowers;
one of them is my home

Like a bee on an apple island
I am waiting for white waters
and apocalypse

I watch you walk against the light

used to someone watching you,
someone you tried to hurt,
someone fingering like a string of beads
a carefully hidden truth about you,
your sexual desire to be offended.
You will wait around a corner
to catch this stalker and then
to feed on his fatal flaw.

All but my true intent

is cloaked in a time hole
but vandals spray it on me
as if they know me better
than I know myself.
To like is my true intent,

to admire and adore,
occasionally to love—
anything else attributed
to me is static,
corruption perhaps
owing to my face's

savage inquiry.
I am not the sum of my data,
I make nothing of yours;
that is why our encounter
is primitive, subject
to misunderstanding and awe.

The offer

If I take away this pain
how will you blaspheme
shibboleths I name?
Tell me, walk straight,
lengthen your stride,
damn your mother
your father & friends,
throw away the hickory
cane of illusions.
I ask nothing else
but that you stop lying
about what happened
when you sent me away.
I am forgiveness
hard as I am to face,
the last obstacle.
After me is peace.

Specks in a lens

I aim the camera at the window
and capture you as you walk behind me,
you know something has happened,
but it's like growing up or getting married—
you don't know what's really going on.

Captor and captive, we never meet,
parent and child, husband and wife,
images in a window, specks in a lens,
we mean so much to each other
and we aren't even friends.

Nobility

Each morning I review the surveillance tapes
in hopes of being able to explain them:
I am mad with their anomalies and submit my resignation
in order to avoid the inevitable unpleasantness.
I should tell you that under subpoena I will take the fifth.

The girl becomes ectoplasmic as if shape memory
fails her under stress, the man sitting there drawing them
is out of the camera's range, but the pages of his notebook
turn in the periphery, the elderly woman is subject to rewind
and all of them enjoy less gravity than they should.

I have failed utterly to keep people from filling rooms,
crushing frail and would-be admirers, sending us
running out to vomit rather than sucking up, failed
in my madness for anomalies, my conviction
that nobility lies in androgyny and unknowing.

Silver halide

Silver halide

You have a silver halide affect:
the world prints out noir
in your presence, its borders
creped in funeral black.

I can thumb through the world
as it were a file, an album,
and I'm an alien examiner.
This world can be cleaned up

with lemon juice and acid;
I'd rather you simply go away
leaving me to colors
and the garishness of life.

I suppose the casual reader
will wonder who you are,
not believe when I say
you orchestrate my dreams

as if without your tinkerings
they'd be mere melodies
offering no lucid moment
for me to listen to them.

Gibberish

What will comfort you?
Imagine being asked,
imagine answering.
How much could we bear
of comfort we describe?
If I were asked I'd say
gibberish, because truth
is combustible,
because life is proof
against the question.
What will comfort me?
Turn your eyes away
while I undress,
open them and see
I could not stay.
Go to the window—
the world will not be there.

Countertenor to detail

You're not my main chance,
it's an elixir lost in me,
cup of sea, glance of stars,
slashing iniquity,
face in a roaring train,
station shut for repairs
abandoned to children
stuck in the moment
they were betrayed.
Countertenor to detail,
that's a main chance worthy
of somebody's cry in the dark.
Refuse to luxuriate
in knowledge, disavow
being right—that is thirst,
rain and honor.

This grand estate

The refugees of your head
scavenge my ruined garden.

I have no work for them,
no papers. They're too late,

I'm tired, but I leave them
this grand estate, the one

that was invisible to you.

Perhaps your enemies

Why is your face screwed up
as if it's working out its rivets
or it's about to blow
the lights of Manhattan out
and shut your enemies in the dark?

Why is the choir
threatening the stained glass
as if in exultation
it knew what you're about
even if you didn't

and if these why's weren't
enough to make God help you
perhaps your enemies will oblige
by scurrying down the drains
leading you to a better light.

Didja

Tell me I wanna know didja think about it?

No your indignance not for a moment
I threw it all away just as it is
what we had together
before the nakba of our birth
when we became strangers
pretending to be human
hoping to encounter
others like us when you
betrayed me to the authorities
and lit out thinking maybe
half of me might be enough
to get by in this half-blind country.

Tell me didja do it?   Do what?

Yes I did and thought about it
long and hard and out of breath
a gaspiness that gets in the way
of hawks turning flickers into splat.
Something else ya wanna know?

Of what use to me are you

or I to you since we
hardly make one
because in quantum physics
I am on the other side of me
from you and in any case
life's a centrifuge
parting me from you
one way or another
at such speeds
we die out of breath?

Prone to becoming you

I

The cowlick at the crown of my head
informs me of your intent
but first my enigma box
with its untranslatable keys
taps out the expressions of my face
in the hope that Bletchley Park
in the name of a greater good
may decipher me so well
that no matter what I make
that electrifies the cowlick
it saves someone huddling
in a basement breaking
to the beat of an angry heart

II

It hardly matters now
the infinitesimal
matters now
three holes in wall
to plaster and sand
Jupiter blocking asteroids
the loud absence
of sexual desire
a dandelion
disturbing the frost
hard frost

putting issues to rest
what matters now
are matters not dire enough before
I hardly matter
I have become prone
to becoming you
and you ululating
as we undress for the stars

The heavens are lonely

Stars collapsed to make me.
Once I emitted light but now
I'm reduced to murmurings.
Do my particles remember
happier days as star beasts?
Does that explain occasions
when even gods smell rancid
and I suspect my dreams
are implants? It explains
nothing because you too
are made of galactic carbon.
We rain on each other, reign
in each other but pretend
we're amnesiacs because
the heavens are lonely
for beasts we helped to be.

Proceeding at my peril

Go snowflake by snowflake
to the station where you'll see
a gunman with a silver 45

Stand behind a stanchion
while he empties his clip on you
crack a joke about his aim

Take the A Train to your grave
but wind up listening to a man
explaining Dean Martin's life

Materialize to make joke
but otherwise remain a shadow
behind the stanchions of the sky

This is the best you can do
oh yes you did fire back
he's bleeding in the snow

a handsome Robert Redford type
people want to believe
with the usual exception of you

Proceed at your peril times five
to some new haven where
the suicide rate is intolerable

Don't forget to wear a face
to reassure the natives
of something you forget

Count your lucky particles
you're averse to shape
except among the intervals

and this is one of them
from that vanished neighborhood
this lurching vomit in your throat

in hurdy-gurdy Brooklyn where
tomorrow's a Breyer's cart
and what's to happen unimaginable

What is more

What is more

What is more

What is more vulgar than identity,
more likely to turn to methane,
rotting stuff of empires,
horde of halfwits,
turning to methane, waiting to explode
as jackboots and kettledrums
tell us how important it is
as we cringe in our windows
wondering why we can't leave it
to the Salvation Army?

Triumphant beast
(After Giordano Bruno)

We are their electrons,
electrons of beasts made of stars.

We are already the zeros of our wake
en route to astronomies up ahead.
We feel our embodiment coming apart,
algebraic ecstasies shuddering
with the comity of becoming something else.

We are a howl of equal signs
and a beast of what is done.

What is happening now?

The child who lived the question must have been killed
even if the evidence suggests he survived.

What is happening now?

A child who lived the question is never satisfied
by evidence or argument or alibi.

Here is what we know of the damned—
we kill them and raise golems
of algebraic ecstasies and equal signs.

We are their mites
obsessed with mightiness,
irritants inciting the smug
and too knowing
to wake to the glory of unknowing
and knowing not nearly enough.

We are their fleas
maddening them.

We are their gnats
blinding them.

We are their lice,
calculus of our poverty,
our doom to be unacceptable
to the godlings examining us.

We are their gluons
binding their phantom quarks.

We are their dots,
their quest in staggering speeds,
essential to asymmetry,
an architecture, a symmetry
incapable of loathing,
therefore divine,
a mathematics no god tinkers,
no eye gets used to,
an innocent beast crashing
in molten hallelujah
through whatever we imagine,
every dot connected, throbbing,
every line traversed,
world without end.

We are their no-see-ums,
infiltrators of our unease,
home invaders fooling around
our underwear, our overweening
satisfaction in our glut.

Are we planets to the suns we choose
whirling at incalculable speeds
to someone else's destination
burning off so much of ourselves
that finally knowledge becomes

another pharmaceutical & we prefer
oblivion to hope?

Clothed in perhaps we live and die,
perhaps the light is more rewarding there
wherever there is and here is as ephemeral
as perhaps, but our clothes do not protect us
from the coldness of our questions.

Is to connect the dots to describe
the arch of triumph, the wormhole
through which beasts not yet imagined
will come in pursuit of a greater sum
than this spiralling pursuit of the sun
trailing arabesques of spent ambition
& proving light does not stand still?

The beast rejoices
to be happily of us,
to blaze with our iniquities.

Rejoice! the beast is us
triumphant in our expulsion
from vaticans and fears
and all the explanations
of our tears, all
the viaticums and horror shows
of being forgiven for being us.

Waiting to wake up

sharing a park bench,
a bite to eat, how
did the movie turn out?
Who needs pay phones
or wristwatches or
any of the desirables
imprudent in this zone?
Will the sky be red
and sailors be warned
when I wake up, will
toilets flush counterclockwise,
gauges be misunderstood?
What language will I speak
or will it be unnecessary
to worry about such things
if I wake up, and if not,
well, that's something, isn't it?

How to be defined

Am I what I remember,
born to be confined,
or the light and carbon
of innumerable ancients,
transponder tasked
with interpreting signals,
a particular creature
of divine conspiracies,
immortal because
I am a borrowed shape,
a habitable name,
nothing if not gone
almost before I came?

Born to wait for snow

everyone impends,
then wounds close
and calm descends.
Each moment melts
in a specific hearth;
the one offense
to this economy
is the waiting.

Almost

I'm busy walking out the door
or flying out the window,
don't call after me
with whisperings of myself,
and if the trouble with this
is that I assume you'll read it
forgive us both all to hell
for thinking that we mattered.

In the cards

Wake up face-blind, listen
to king queen jack shuffling
in a dealer's hand, blot out
one two three or more and go
about as if nothing happened
knowing who did this to you
and is now as out of reach
as when you were a child.

You may even make love to them
sharpened by hatred,
they may even respond
as if this were not the necropolis
you flit around at night;
by morning they will pocket
more of the ghouls who depend
on you to offend them.

Are the dead now your friends?

Too big, too loud, too bright

Too big too loud too bright too close

life without special effects
without shadows or give
would such a life resemble
vanishing bit by bit into mirrors
or seeing our minds undress
not remembering having cojones
or would a thousand addresses
flood into your head
and you remembering what happened
at each of them when you still cast a shadow
and could dramatize
the behavior of crooks loved ones
inveiglers and other familiars?

You're not breaking down, you're catching on
to a savagely televised story being untold

As they say in Argentina

To look but not acquire
is to pass by unconsumed
by what's already rotting
and would have detained
if you had not admired
as only an old man could

I say old man but could
have said a dervish or
a disappeared as they
say in Argentina but
all I mean is one whose love
has sombered in the fire

The Boylan bottle

One day you're staring at a Boylan Company label,
next day you're something called dead
& a lifetime is not enough time to be amazed
that on the other side of the Boylan bottle
The New York Times seems to know what it's about
& all you have in common with the Times
is that you've always been on the other side
with some Boylan standing in the way.

Plummet

Can you get me out of here?

How much will you kill me for it?

I'm thinking, thinking, that is my allure,
thinking how to kill you for what I need,
how to disassemble you,
how to kill in you what I need,
thinking till the plum rots,
the pit cracks and the thought goes bad,
and you on the other side of the city
don't even know where here is
or what it costs, and yet you had that look
of the angel I was born to kill,
even in my old age trapped in an elevator,
that look that maybe you can get me out of here.

My aperture is stuck wide open

my image in the window rebuffs the lens,
I've always stood in the way of inquiry

I'm all that stands between you
and who you plan to incinerate

no one's fingers have ever passed
this quaking child's inspection

already cursed for letting light in
I am set to let harm's way begin

In its otherness the camera does not see
the eucharist celebrated by the eye

and yet in its religious accidents
it tickles us with its heresies

nothing filters out your light

Black light

You are black light, you see through varnish.
I have followed you here to this loft
where the loot of pretense is stored
to feast on what is underneath the gloss,
to die of all sorts of things, not least
delight, and finally to ascend
through the painted skylight to the arms
of one who never wished to let me go,
one who accompanied me here disguised
as another, one whose priestesses bear
the black light believers fear.

Bocaccio tried

Yours is not one of the 10,000 odors
humans can smell, so one of us,
well, not to put too fine a point,
is suspect of unimaginable things.

Bocaccio tried to imagine them—
Dante Alighieri, JRR Tolkien,
and other perps, but will you please
try to walk, not skitter or scud?

Let's make a star beast if we meet again,
one to shake galaxies off her hide,
toss black holes around and wind
civilizations around her thumb.

Alyssum and ozone

I cannot bring events to ground.

You smell alyssum, I smell ozone.

My body is a heath of burnt grass.

Lightning will strike twice, no one
is fast enough to change that,
not even shapeshifters.

Here is no intolerable knowledge.

Savvy is life in the crosshairs,
seeing around corners,
being surefooted enough
to know black mambas wait
in the cane fields of desire.

I can make the sniper ill,
I can shoot up love
to thwart suffocation,
but lightning seeking ground,
causing me to tingle, that might be

a chariot coming for to take me home,
an angel reaching out to me,
shutting down the crosshairs
I sensed in the cradle, and that
is hallelujah, kingdom come.

Primavera is watching you

Beauty may uprear as Lenten rose
but it's as old as light from stars
& artifactual only in the sense
it morphs to the witness of admirers
& even as a plastic art explores
the nature of the beguiled

Primavera is watching you
even as you watch the girl
drying off the gaze of others
in the corner of the gallery;
Botticelli sends you his regards
and wishes to remind you

You are swarmed by messengers
who touch you here & there
for a reason. The hellebore in the snow
spent last night conferring
with them about what you ought to do
now that it sinks in
no one's beauty is ever new

Dye run

if you sneak up on my six
I'll fuck up your pixels;
you'll never hang straight

you didn't get this yes you did
& you pretended she
never said it yes she did

not in so many words
but withholding of a tit
& blue hauteur

that dyed your skin
Pictish to the Romans'
seeming civilization

her pixels deranged themselves,
you just took the rap
& then one morning in the shower

you saw the dye run off
between your toes
as if you'd never lived

The tree saw

me you and you me inflicting pain
God's tree saw clearing
a sunfall in the woods
where elementals carry on
a night or two then carry off
us two burnt offerings

wouldn't that be
suitable leave-taking
for two outlaws who saw too much
& took in the toxins of the mine
such dutiful canaries
and wouldn't we
with our minds' last gasp
pluck stars from trees

Temenos nakedly

And then the preacher said
life is just a baggage claim,
I swear to God he said
a name is the first obscenity,
enter Temenos nakedly
or it may as well be Canarsie.
And when we looked up
it was just a recording
going on and on. Sleep
is not absolution, it said,
but the scent of that one mind
for which we're born desperate
and ecstasy is remembrance,
I swear to God it said
go for that loaf of bread,
don't ever come back,
and when they ask for your name
say you've forgotten it
and eventually you will.
Who will go along with this?
No one, but you will be one
with the crime you were meant to commit.

To dance with ghouls

We've learned to be famous,
ride a white horse, pass
through keyholes, kiss ass
skillfully, dance with ghouls
in cheeky cemeteries
where words and images
go to rot,
                    learned
fame is more convenient
than it used to be, more practical
than evolutionary things.
You can grab it by the balls,
rig the market for it, and all
you have to be is quick,
                    but when
you hear breathing in the walls,
a rustle in the mind, then
you kiss the hands of ghouls,
thank them for the dance,
rejoin the carbon thread
knowing nothing is ever dead.

Worry-me's in the baseboards

voices in the wall speak the language
we speak to expunge. My feet are cold,
my body heat escapes
in balls of strung words, my breath
is an icicle pointed at the head
of the unwary, and I strip
to dance with snow devils
on the rumps of old ambitions.

I don't know what I feel to prompt
the babel in the walls, what I say
to agitate the worry-me's,
but when I read a poem to a crowded room
I come home with its anima,
caught in a cobweb of allures.
I belong to the voices in the wall
from millions of miles away
and this is all I can think to say.

I would like to wake in a formal garden

butterflies in a silver sea at my feet.
If you wish this for me I will remember you.
Let us make no further plans. Developments
will be the consequence of butterflies,
names will turn to pollen,
and I will walk away.

No maze, I will be done with that,
but I would like an arboretum to shelter in
when thunder shakes the ground and lightning
limns the true shape of ideas. I will fade
and fall apart, I will not intrude or possess.
After a long while smiling in the evening
I will walk away.

Nothing will ever be true again,
or false, and whatever I understood
will become light taking its time
to arrive upon the face of one
who seeing me across the street
will remember a great bonfire
before doubts closed in.

Ascendance

Certainty of you
filament of you
rustle of lift
lilt of light
You
scent's nostalgia
are?
numinous.
There is
no other question.